Anonymous

A Narrative of the Indian and Civil Wars in Virginia

Anonymous

A Narrative of the Indian and Civil Wars in Virginia

ISBN/EAN: 9783337222338

Printed in Europe, USA, Canada, Australia, Japan

Cover: Foto ©ninafisch / pixelio.de

More available books at **www.hansebooks.com**

A NARRATIVE

OF THE

INDIAN AND CIVIL WARS

IN

VIRGINIA,

IN THE YEARS 1675 AND 1676.

PUBLISHED FROM THE ORIGINAL MANUSCRIPT, IN THE FIRST
VOLUME (SECOND SERIES) OF THE COLLECTIONS OF
THE MASSACHUSETTS HISTORICAL SOCIETY.

BOSTON:
PRINTED BY JOHN ELIOT, No. 5 COURT STREET.
1814.

NO 10   FEBRUARY 1898
COLONIAL TRACTS
Published by GEORGE P HUMPHREY
ROCHESTER N Y

WASHINGTON, December 20, 1812.

Dear Sir—The manuscript copy of Bacon and Ingram's Rebellion was found among the papers of the late Captain Nathaniel Burwell of King William county. I have not been able to obtain many particulars from his family relative to it.

At the close of the war he heard of its existence in an old and respectable family of the northern neck of Virginia, and procured it for his amusement; he entertained no doubt of its antiquity, and valued it on that account.

From the appearance of the work, the minute and circumstantial detail of facts, the orthography, and the style, I am perfectly satisfied his opinion was correct. I hope it will be found worthy of a place in the valuable collections of the society to which you belong.

Permit me to offer my best wishes for the success of your labors. Yours, respectfully,

WILLIAM A. BURWELL,

of Virginia.

THE INDIAN PROCEEDINGS. *

. . . .

for their own security. They found that their store was too short to endure a long siege, without making empty bellies, and that empty bellies make weak hearts, which always makes an unfit serving man to wait upon the god of war. Therefore they were resolved, before their spirits were down, to do what they could to keep their stores up, as opportunity should befriend them ; and although they were by the law of arms (as the case now stood) prohibited the hunting of wild deer, they resolved to see what good might be done by hunting tame horses, which trade became their sport so long that those who came on horseback to the siege began to fear they should be compelled to trot home on foot, and glad if they escaped so, too, for these beleaguered blades made so many sallies, and the besiegers kept such negligent guard, that there were very few days passed without some remarkable mischief. But what can hold out always ? Even stone walls yield to the not-to-be gainsaid summons of time. And although it is said that the Indians do the least mind their bellies (as being content with a little) of any people in the world, yet now their bellies began to mind them, and their stomachs, too, which began to be more inclinable to peace than war, which was the cause (no more horse-flesh being to be had) that they sent out six of their Wœrowances (chief men) to commence a treaty. What the articles were that they brought along with them to treat of I do not know, but certainly they were so unacceptable to the English that they caused the commissioners' brains to be knocked out for dictating so badly to their tongues, which yet, it is possible, expressed more reason than the English had to prove the lawfulness of this action, being diametrical to the law of arms.

* We regret that the beginning of this manuscript is missing, and that several parts were so much torn that it became necessary to leave vacant spaces. Where the expression is uncertain, but the page not wholly disfigured, we have used *italic letters.*—Ed.

This strange action put those in the fort to their trumps, having thus lost some of their prime court cards without a fair dealing. They could not tell what interpretation to put upon it (nay, indeed, nobody else), and very fain they would *understand* why those whom they sent out with a *view to supplicate* a peace should be worse dealt with than those who were sent out with a sword to denounce a war ; but *no one* could be got to make inquiry into the reason of this, . . which put them upon a resolution to forsake their *station*, and not to expostulate the cause any further. Having *made* this resolution, and destroyed all things in the fort that might be serviceable to the English, they boldly, undiscovered, slip through the league (leaving the English to prosecute the siege as Schogin's wife brooded the eggs that the fox had sucked), in the passing of which they knocked ten men on the head who lay carelessly asleep in their way.

Now, although it might be said that the Indians went their ways empty-handed, in regard they had left all their plunder and wealth behind them in the fort, yet it cannot be thought that they went away empty-hearted, for though that was pretty well drained from its former courage through those inconveniences that they had been subjected to by the siege, yet in the room thereof, rather than the venticles should lie void, they had stowed up so much malice, intermixed with a resolution of revenge for the affront that the English had put upon them in killing their messengers of peace, that they resolved to commence a most barbarous and most bloody war.

The besiegers having spent a great deal of ill-employed time in pecking at the husk, and now finding the shell open, and missing the expected prey, did not a little wonder what was become of the lately impounded Indians, who, though at present they could not be seen, yet it was not long before they were heard of, and felt, too, for in a very short time they had, in a most inhuman manner, murdered no less than sixty innocent people, noways guilty of any actual injury done to these ill-discerning, brutish heathen. By the blood of these poor souls, they thought that the wandering ghosts of those their commissioners, before mentioned, might be atoned and laid down to take their repose in the dismal shades of death, and they, at present, not obliged for to prosecute any further revenge.

Therefore, to prove whether the English were as ready for a peace as themselves, they send their remonstrance in the name of their *chief*, taken by an English interpreter, unto the governor of Virginia, with whom he expostulates in this sort : What *was* it that moved him to take up arms against him, his *professed* friend, in the behalf of the Marylanders, his professed enemies, contrary to that league made between him and himself ? declares as well his own as subjects' grief to find the Virginians, of friends, without any cause given to become his foes, and to be so eager in their groundless quarrel as to pursue the chase into another's dominions ; complains that his messengers of peace were not only murdered by the English, but the fact countenanced by the governor's connivance, for which, seeing no other way to be satisfied, he had revenged himself by killing ten for one of the Virginians, such being the disproportion between his great men murdered and those by his command slain ; that now, this being done, if that his honor would allow him a valuable satisfaction for the damage he had sustained by the war, and no more concern himself in the Marylanders' quarrel, he was content to renew and confirm the ancient league of amity, otherways himself and those whom he had engaged to his interests, and their own, were resolved to fight it out to the last man.

These proposals not being assented to by the English, as being derogatory and point blank both to honor and interest, these Indians draw in others, formerly in subjection to the Virginians, to their 'aid, which, being conjoined, in separate and united parties, they daily committed abundance of unguarded and unrevenged murders upon the Cruelties of the Indians. English, which they perpetrated in a most barbarous and horrid manner. By which means abundance of the frontier plantations became either depopulated by the Indian settlers or deserted by the planters' fears, who were compelled to forsake their abodes to find security for their lives, which they were not to part with in the hands of the Indians but under the worst of torments. For these brutish and inhuman brutes, lest their cruelties might not be thought cruel enough, devised a hundred ways to torture and torment those poor souls with, whose wretched fate it was to fall into their unmerciful hands. For some, before they would deprive them of their lives, they

would take a great deal of time to deprive them first of their skins, and if their life had not, through the anguish of their pain, forsaken their tormented bodies, they *with their clubs knocked out their teeth* (or some instrument), tear off the nails of *their hands* and their toes, which put the poor sufferer to a woeful *condition*. One was *prepared for the flames at Jamestown*, who endured much, but found means to escape . . . .
. . . . for lest their deaths should be attributed to some more merciful hands than theirs, to put all out of question, they would leave some of those brutish marks upon their defenceless bodies, that they might testify it could be none but they who had committed the fact.

And now it was that the poor, distressed, and doubly afflicted planters began to curse and execrate that ill-managed business at the fort. Their cries were reiterated again and again, both to God and to man for relief. But no appearance of long-wished-for safety arising in the horizon of their hopes, they were ready, could they have told which way, to leave all and forsake the colony rather than to stay and be exposed to the cruelties of the barbarous heathen.

At last it was concluded as a good expedient for to put the country in a good degree of safety, to plant forts upon the frontiers, thinking thereby to put a stop to the Forts to be built. Indians' excursions, which, after the expense of a great deal of time and charge, being finished, came short of the designed ends. For the Indians quickly found out where the mouse-traps were set, and for what purpose, and so resolved to keep out of the way of their danger, which they might easy enough do without any detriment to their designs. For though hereby they were compelled to go, it is possible, a little about, yet they never thought much of their Not valued by the Indians. labor so long as they were not debarred from doing mischief, which was not in the power of these forts to prevent. For if that the English did at any time know that there were more ways into the wood than one to kill deer, the Indians found more, a thousand out of the wood, to kill men, and not come near the danger of the forts either.

The small good that was by most expected, and now by them experienced, from those useless fabrics (or castles, *if so we say*), excited a marvelous discontent among the people.

Some thought the charge would be great, and the benefit little.
. . . . It *rent the hearts of many* that they should be compelled to work all day, nay, all the year for to reward those
mole-catchers at the fort, nobody knew for what, and at night
could not find a place of safety to lie down in to rest their weary
bones, for fear they should be shattered all to pieces by the
Indians; upon which consideration they thought it best to
petition the downfall of these useless, and like to be, chargeable
fabrics, from whose continuance they could neither expect profit
nor safety.

But for the effecting this business they found themselves
under a very great disadvantage, for though it may be
more easy to cast down than erect well-cemented The forts dis-
structures, yet the rule doth not hold good in all cases. English.
For it is to be understood that these forts were contrived either by the sole command of the governor, or otherwise
by the advice of those whose judgments, in these affairs, he
approved of, either of which was now, they being done, his
own immediate act, as they were done in his name, which to
have undone at the simple request of the people had been in
effect to have undone the repute he always held in the people's
judgment for a wise man ; and better that they should suffer
some small inconveniences than that he should be accounted
less discerning than those who till now were counted more
than half blind. Besides, how should he satisfy his honor of
the undertakers of the work. If the people's petition be
granted, they must be disappointed, which would be little less
than an undoing to them also in their expectation of profit to
be raised from the work. Hereby the people quickly found
themselves in an error, when that they apprehended what a
strong foundation the forts were erected upon, honor and profit,
against which all their sapping and mining had no power to
overturn. They having no other ingredients to make up their
fireworks with but prayers and misspent tears and entreaties,
which having vented to no purpose, and finding their condition
every whit as bad, if not worse, as before the forts were made,
they resolved to . . . . .

BACON'S PROCEEDINGS.

THE *people chose Col. Bacon their general, which post he accepted.*
He was a man of quality and merit, brave and eloquent,
became much endeared, not so much for what he had
yet done as the cause of their affections, as for
what they expected he would do to deserve their
devotion ; while with no common zeal they sent up
their reiterated prayers, first to himself and next to Heaven,
that he may become their guardian angel, to protect them from
the cruelties of the Indians, against whom this gentleman had
a perfect antipathy.

(marginal note: Bacon appears against the Indians.)

It seems that at the first rise of the war this gentleman had
made some overtures unto the governor for a commission to go
and put a stop to the Indians' proceedings. But the governor
at present, either not willing to commence the quarrel (on his
part) till more suitable reasons presented for to urge his more
severe prosecution of the same, against the heathen, or that he
doubted Bacon's temper, as he appeared popularly inclined ; a
constitution not being consistent with the times or the people's
dispositions, being generally discontented for want of timely
provisions against the Indians, or for annual impositions laid
upon them, too great, as they said, for them to bear, and against
which they had some considerable time complained
without the least redress ; for these, or some other
reasons, the governor refused to comply with Bacon's
proposals. Which he, looking upon as undervaluing

(marginal note: Bacon advanceth against the Indians.)

as well to his parts as a disparagement to his pretensions, he,
in some elated and passionate expressions, sware, commission
or no commission, the next man or woman he heard of that
should be killed by the Indians, he would go out against them,
though but twenty men would adventure the service with him.
Now it so unhappily fell out that the next person that the
Indians did kill was one of his own family.   Whereupon,
having got together about seventy or ninety persons, most
good housekeepers, well armed, and seeing that he could not
legally procure a commission (after some strugglings with the
governor), *some of his best friends* who *condemned* his enter-
prises, he applies himself.   .   .   .   .   .   .

The governor could not bear this insolent deportment of Bacon, *and spake freely against him and condemned his proceedings.* Which . . instead of seeking means to appease his anger, they devised means to increase it, by framing specious pretences which they grounded upon the boldness of Bacon's actions and the people's affections. They began, some of them, to have Bacon's merits in mistrust, as a luminary that threatened an eclipse to their rising glories ; for though he was but a young man, yet they found that he was master and owner of those induements which constitute a complete man, as to intrinsical wisdom to apprehend and discretion to choose. By which embellishments, if he should continue in the governor's favor, of seniors they might become juniors, while their younger brother, through the nimbleness of his wit, might steal away that blessing which they accounted their own by birthright. This rash proceeding of Bacon, if it did not undo himself by his failing in the enterprise, might chance to undo them in the affections of the people ; which to prevent, they thought it conduceable to their interest and establishment for to get the governor in the mind to proclaim him a rebel, as knowing that once being done, since it could not be done but in and by the governor's name, it must needs breed bad blood between Bacon and Sir William, not easily to be purged. For though Sir William might forgive what Bacon as yet had acted, yet it might be questionable whether Bacon might forget what Sir William had done. However, according to their desires, Bacon and all his adherents was proclaimed a rebel May the 29th, and forces raised to reduce him to his duty ; with which the governor advanced from the middle plantation * to find him out and if need was to fight him, if the Indians had not knocked him and those that were with him in the head, as some were in hope they had done, and which by some was earnestly desired.

After some days the governor retracts his march, a journey of some thirty or forty miles, to meet the assembly now ready to set down at our metropolis, while Bacon in the meanwhile meets with the Indians, upon whom he falls with abundance of resolution and gallantry (as his own party relates it) in their fastness, killing a

Forces raised to reduce Bacon.

Bacon meets with the Indians.

* Williamsburg. See Beverly's History of Virginia.

great many and blowing up their magazine of arms and powder to a considerable quantity, if *we may judge from himself,* no less than four thousand weight. This being done, and *all his* provisions spent, he returns home, and *while here* submits himself to be chosen burgess of the county in which he did live, contrary to his *qualifications* take him as he was formerly one of the council of state or, as he was now a proclaimed rebel. However, he applies himself to the performance of that trust reposed in him by the people, if he might be admitted into the house. But this not faring according to his desire, though according to his expectation, and he remaining in his sloop, then at anchor before the town, in which was about thirty gentle-

Bacon taken prisoner.

men besides himself, he was there surprised and made prisoner with the rest, some being put into irons, in which condition they remained some time, till all things were fitted for the trial. Which being brought

Brought upon his trial and acquitted.

to a day of hearing, before the governor and council, Bacon was not only acquitted and pardoned all misdemeanors, but restored to the council table as before ; and not only this, but promised to have a commission signed the Monday following (this was Saturday),

June 10 promised a commission.

as general for the Indian war, to the universal satisfaction of the people, who passionately desired the same, witnessed by the general acclamations of all then in town.

And here who can do less than wonder at the mutable and impermanent deportments of that blind goddess, Fortune, who in the morning leads man with disgraces, and ere night crowns him with honors ; sometimes depressing, and again elevating, as her fickle humor is to smile or frown, of which this gentleman's fate was a kind of epitome in the several vicissitudes and changes he was subjected to in a very few days. For in the morning, before his trial, he was in his enemy's hopes and friends' fears judged for to receive the guerdon due to a rebel (and such he was proclaimed to be), and ere night crowned the darling of the people's hopes and desires, as the only man fit in Virginia to put a stop to the bloody resolution of the heathen. And yet again, as a fuller manifestation of fortune's inconstancy, within two or three days the people's hopes and his desires were both frustrated by the governor's refusing to sign the promised commission. At which being disgusted, though he dissembled the same as well as he could, he begs leave of the governor to dispense with his services at the council table, to visit his *wife, who, as she had informed him, was indisposed,* which request the governor (after some contest with his own thoughts) granted, contrary to the advice of some about him, who suspected Bacon's designs, and that it was not so much his lady's sickness as the troubles of a distempered mind which caused him to withdraw to his own house, and that this was the truth, which in a few days was manifested, when that he returned to town with five hundred men in arms.

(margin: The governor refuses to sign the commission. Bacon disgusted.)

The governor did not want intelligence of Bacon's designs, and therefore sent out his summons for York train-bands to reinforce his guards then at town. But the time was so short, not above twelve hours' warning, and those that appeared at the rendezvous made such a slender number, that under four ensigns there was not mustered above one hundred soldiers, and not one-half of them sure neither, and all so sluggish in their march, that before they could reach town, by a great deal, Bacon had entered the same and by force obtained a commission, calculated to the height of his own desires. With which commission being invested, such as it was, he makes ready his provisions, fills up his companies to the designed number (five hundred in all), and so applies himself to those services the country expected from him. And, first, for the securing the same against the excursions of the Indians in his absence, and such might be expected, he commissioned several persons such as he could confide in, in every respective county, with select companies of well-armed men, to ravage the forests, thickets, swamps, and all such suspected places where Indians might have any shelter for the doing of mischief. Which proceedings of his put so much courage into the planters that they began to apply themselves to their accustomed employments in their plantations, which till now they durst not do, for fear of being knocked in the head, as God knows too many were before these orders were observed.

(margin: Bacon returns to town at the head of five hundred men, and forceth a commission.)

14

While the general (for so was Bacon now denominated by virtue of his commission) was sedulous in these affairs, and fitting his provisions, about the head of York river, in order to his advance against the Indians, the governor was steering quite different courses. He was once more persuaded (but for what reasons not visible) to proclaim Bacon a rebel again, and now, since his absence afforded an advantage to raise the country upon him, so soon as he should return tired and exhausted by his toil and labor in the Indian war. For the putting this council in execution, the governor steps over in Gloster county (a place the best replenished for men, arms, and affection of any county in Virginia), all which the governor summons to give him a meeting at a place and day assigned; where being met, according to summons, the governor's proposals was so much disrelished by the whole convention, that they all disbanded to their own abodes, after their promise passed to stand by and assist the governor against all those who should go about to wrong his person or debase his authority ; unto which promise they annexed or subjoined several reasons why they thought it not convenient at present to declare themselves against Bacon, as he was now advancing against the common enemy, who had in a most barbarous manner murdered some hundreds of their dear brethren and countrymen, and would, if not prevented by God and the endeavors of good men, do their utmost for to cut off the whole colony.

Therefore did they think that it would be a thing The Gloster men's protestation. inconsistent with right reason if that they, in this desperate conjuncture of time, should go and engage themselves one against another ; from the result of which proceedings, nothing could be expected but ruin and destruction unto both, to the one and other party, since it might reasonably be conceived that while they should be exposing their breasts against one another's weapons, the barbarous and common enemy, who would make his advantages by our disadvantages, should be upon their backs to knock out their brains. But if it should so happen as they did hope would never happen, that the general, after the Indian war was finished, should attempt anything against his honor's person or government, that they would rise up in arms, with a joint consent, for the preservation of both.

Since the governor could obtain no more, he was at present to rest himself contented with this, while those who had advised him to these undertakings were not a little dissatisfied to find the event not answer their expectations. But he at present, seeing there was no more to be done, since he wanted a power to have that done which was esteemed the main of the affairs now in hand to be done, namely, the gaining of the Gloster men, to do what he would have done, he thought it best to do what he had a power to do, and that was once more to proclaim Bacon a traitor, which was performed in all public places of meetings in these parts. The noise of which proclamation, after that it had passed the admiration of all that were not acquainted with the reasons that moved his honor to do what he had now done, soon reached the general's ears, not yet stopped up from listening to apparent dangers.

This strange and unexpected news put him, and some with him, shrewdly to their trumps, believing that a few such deals or shuffles (call them what you please) might quickly wring the cards and game, too, out his hand. He perceived that he was fallen like the corn between the stones, so that if he did not look the better about him he might chance be ground to powder. He knew that to have a certain enemy in his front, and more than uncertain friends in his rear, portended no great security from a violent death, and that there could be no great difference between his being wounded to death in his breast with bows and arrows or in the back with guns and musket bullets. He did see that there was an absolute necessity of destroying the Indians for the preservation of the English, and that there was some care to be taken for his own and soldiers' safety, otherwise that work must be ill done where the laborers are made cripples and compelled, instead of a sword, to betake themselves to a crutch.

It vexed him to the heart (as he was heard to say) for to think that while he was hunting wolves, tigers, and foxes, which daily destroyed our harmless sheep and lambs, that he, and those with him, should be pursued, with a full cry, as a more savage or a no less ravenous beast. But to put all out of doubt, and himself in some degree of safety, since he could not tell but that some whom he left behind might not more

16

desire his death than to hear that by him the Indians were
destroyed, he forthwith (after a short consultation held with
some of his soldiers) countermarches his army, and in a trice
came up with them at the middle plantation, * a place situated
in the very heart of the country.

The first thing that Bacon fell upon (after that he had settled
himself at the middle plantation), was *prepare his* remonstrance,
and that as well against a certain *anonymous* paper of the
twenty-ninth of May, as in answer to the governor's proclamation. Putting both papers upon *these declarations, he asks*
whether persons wholly devoted to their king and country,
haters of all sinister and by-respects, aiming only at their
country's good, and endeavoring to the *utmost of their* power,
to the hazard of their lives and fortunes, *that they might* destroy
those that are in arms against their king and *country*, men who
never plotted, contrived, nor endeavored *any* indiscretion,
detriment, or wrong of any of his majesty's *subjects*, in their
lives, names, fortunes, or estates, can deserve the appellation
of rebels and traitors.

He cites the whole country to testify his and his soldiers'
peaceable behavior ; upbraids some in authority with the meanness of their parts ; others, now wealthy, with the meanness
of their estates when they first came into the country ; and
questions by what just ways or means they have obtained the
same, and whether they have not been the sponges
Bacon's dec-
laration. that have sucked up and devoured the common
treasury ? Questions what arts, sciences, schools
of learning, or manufactures have been promoted by any now
in authority ? Justifies his aversion, in general, against the
Indians, upbraids the governor for maintaining their quarrel
(though never so unjust) against the Christian rights and
interests ; his refusing to admit an Englishman's oath against an
Indian, when that Indian's word would be sufficient proof against
an Englishman. Saith something against the governor about
the beaver trade as being a monopoly. . . . . .
Arraigns one Colonel Cole's assertion *for saying* that the
English are bound to protect the Indians at the hazard of their
blood ; and so concludes with an appeal to king and parliament,

* Williamsburg.

where he *has no doubt* that his and the people's cause will be impartially heard.

After this manner the game begins. *This declaration* of Bacon was the prelude to the following chapter. . . .

His next work was to invite all that had any regard to themselves or love to their country, their wives, children, and other relations, to give him a meeting at his quarters, at a day named, then and there to consider how to put the country into some degree of safety, and to endeavor to stop those imminent dangers now threatening the destruction of the whole colony, through the bloody proceedings of the Indians ; and, as he said, by Sir William's doting and irregular actings. Desiring of them not to sit still in this common time of calamity, with their hands in their bosoms, or as unconcerned spectators stand gazing upon their approaching ruin and not lend a hand to squelch those flames now likely to consume them and theirs to ashes. According to the summons, most of the prime gentlemen of these parts, whereof some were of the council of state, gave Bacon a meeting at his quarters at the assigned time. Where being met (after a long harangue by him made, much of the nature of and to explain the summons), he desired them to take the same so far into their consideration that there might, by their wisdom, some expedient be found out, as well for the country's security against Sir William's irregular proceedings as that he and the army might unmolestedly prosecute the Indian war. Adding, that neither himself nor those under his command thought it a thing consistent with reason or common sense to advance against the common enemy and in the meantime want assurance, when they had done the work abroad, not to have their throats cut when they should return home by those who had set them to work. Being confident that Sir William and some others with him, through a sense of their unwarrantable actions, would do what was possible to be done, not only to destroy himself, but others privy to their knavery, now engaged in the Indian service with him.

After that Bacon had urged what he thought meet for the better carrying on of those affairs now hammering in his head, it was concluded by the whole convention that for the establishing of the general and army in a consistency of safety, and that as well upon his march against the Indians as when he should return from the service, and also for the keeping of the country in peace in his absence, that there should be a test or recognition drawn and subscribed to by the whole country, which should oblige them, and every of them, not to be aiding or assisting Sir William Berkeley (for now he would not afford him the title of governor) in any sort to the molestation, hindrance, or detriment of the general and army. This being assented to, the clerk of the assembly was ordered to put the same into form. Which, while he was doing, the general would needs have another branch added to the former, viz., that the people should not only be obliged not to be aiding Sir W. B. against the general, but the force of this recognition should be obliged to rise in arms against him if he with armed forces should offer to resist the general or disturb the country's peace in his absence, and not only so (but to make the engagement *a-la-mode* rebellion), he would have it added, that if any forces should be sent out of England at the request of Sir William, or otherwise to his aid, that they were likewise to be opposed till such time as the country's cause should be sent *home* and reported to his most sacred majesty.

An oath pro-jected.

These two last branches of this bugbear did marvelously startle the people, especially the very last of all; yet to give the general satisfaction how willing they were to give him all the security that lay in their power, they seemed willing to subscribe the two first as they stood single, but not to any if the last must be joined with them. But the general used or urged a great many reasons for signing the whole engagement, as it was presented in the three conjoined branches, otherwise no security could be expected, neither to the country, army, nor himself. Therefore he was resolved, if that they would not do what he did judge so reasonable and necessary to be done, in and about the premises, that he would surrender up his commission to the assembly and let the country find some other servants to go abroad and do their work.

For, says he, it is to be considered that Sir William hath already proclaimed me a rebel, and it is not unknown to himself that I both can and shall charge him with no less than treason. And it is not only myself that must be and is concerned in what shall be

Bacon's reasons for the taking the oath.

charged against him, but several gentlemen in the country
besides, who now are and ever will be against his interest;
and of those that shall adhere to his illegal proceedings, of
which he being more than ordinarily sensible, it cannot in
common reason be otherwise conceived but that he, being
assisted by those forces now employed, that they shall not be
wholly employed to the destruction of all those capable to
frame an accusation against him to his sacred majesty.
Neither can it be reasonably apprehended that he will ever
condescend to any friendly accommodation with those that
shall subscribe to all or any part of this engagement, unless
such or such persons shall be surrendered up to his mercy to
be proceeded against as he shall see fit; and then how many
or few those may be, whom he shall make choice of to be sent
into the other world that he may be rid of his fears in this,
may be left to consideration.

Many things were, by many of those who were of this meeting, urged pro and con concerning the taking or not taking of
the engagement. But such was the resolute temper of the
general against all reasoning to the contrary, that the whole
must be swallowed or else no good would be done. In the
urging of which he used such subtile and specious pretences;
sometimes for the pressing and not to be dispensed with necessity, in regard of those fears the whole colony was subjected
to through the daily murders perpetrated by the Indians, and
then again opening the harmlessness of the oath, as he would
have it to be, and which he managed solely against a great
many of those counted the wisest men in the country, with so
much art and sophistical dexterity that at length there was
little said by any against the same. Especially when the
gunner of York fort arrived, imploring aid to secure the same
against the Indians, adding that there were a great number of
poor people fled into it for protection, which could not be unless
there was some speedy course taken to reinforce the said fort
with munition and arms, otherwise it and those fled to it
would go near hand to fall into the power of the heathen.

The general was somewhat startled at this news, and
accordingly expostulated the same, how it could possibly be
that the most considerable fortress in the country should be
in danger to be surprised by the Indians. But being told that

the governor, the day before, had caused all the arms and ammunition to be conveyed out of the fort into his own vessel, with which he was sailed forth of the country, as it was thought, it is strange to think what impression this story made upon the people's apprehensions. In earnest, this action did stagger a great many, otherwise well inclined to Sir William, who could not tell what constructions to put upon it. However, this was no great disadvantage to Bacon's designs; he knew well enough how to make his advantages out of this, as well as he did out of the Gloster business, before mentioned, by framing and stumping out to the people's apprehensions what commentaries or interpretations he pleased, upon the least oversight by the governor committed ; which he managed with so much cunning and subtilty that the people's minds became quickly flexible and apt to receive any impression or similitude that his arguments should represent to their ill-discerning judgments ; insomuch that the oath became now more smooth and glib to be swallowed, even by those

The oath taken. who had the greatest repugnance against it; so that there were no more discourses used either for restrictions or enlargements. Only this salvo was granted unto those who would claim the benefit of it (and some did so), yet not expressed in the written copy, viz., that if there was anything in the same of such dangerous consequence that it might taint the subscribers' allegience, that then they should stand absolved from all and every part of the said oath ; unto which the general gave his consent (and certainly he had too much cunning to deny or gainsay it) saying, " God forbid that it should be otherwise meant or intended ;" adding that himself (and army, by his command) had, some few days before, taken the oath of allegience, therefore it could not rationally be imagined that either himself or they would go about to act or do anything contrary to the meaning of the same.

Bad ware requires a dark store, while sleek and pounce inveigles the chapman's judgment. Though the first subscribers were indulged the liberty of entering their exceptions against the strict letter of the oath, yet others who were to take the same before the respective justices of peace in their several jurisdictions were not to have the same latitude. For the power of affording cautions and exceptions was solely in

21

the imposer, not in those who should hereafter administer the
oath, whereby the aftertakers were obliged to swallow the
same, though it might hazard their chokening, as it stood in
the very letter thereof. Neither can I apprehend what benefit
could possibly accrue more unto those who were indulged the
aforesaid privilege than to those who were debarred the same,
since both subscribed the engagement as it stood in the letter,
not as it was in the meaning of the subscriber. It is true,
before God and their own consciences it might be pleadable,
but not at the bar of human proceedings, without a favorable
interpretation put upon it by those who were to be the judges.

While Bacon was contriving and imposing this illegal oath,
for to secure himself against the governor, the governor was
no less solicitous to find out means to secure himself against
Bacon. Therefore, as the only place of security
within the colony to keep out of Bacon's reach, he Sir William
sails over to Accomack. This place is sequestered mack. salls for Acco-
from the main part of Virginia through the inter-
position of the great Bay of Chesapeake, being itself an isthmus
and commonly called the eastern shore. It is bounded on the
east with the main ocean, and on the southwest with the aforesaid bay, which runs up into the country navigable for the
biggest ships more than two hundred and forty miles, and so,
consequently, not approachable from the other parts of Virginia
but by water, without surrounding the head of the said bay,—
a labor of toil, time, and danger, in regard of the way and
habitations of the Indians.

It was not long before Bacon was informed where the
governor had taken sanctuary, neither was he ignorant what
it was that moved him to do what he had done. He did also
apprehend that as he had found the way out, he could, when
he saw his own time, find the way in again ; and though he
went forth with an empty hand, he might return
with a full fist. For the preventing of which, as he Bland and
thought, he despatched away one Esquire Bland, a to Accomack. Carver sent
gentleman of an active and stirring disposition, and
no great admirer of Sir William's goodness ; and with him in
commission one Captain Carver, a person acquainted with
navigation, and one, as they say, indebted to Sir William
before he died for his life upon a double account, with forces

in two ships, either to block Sir William up in Accomack, or otherwise to inveigle the inhabitants, thinking that all the country, like the friar in the bush, must needs be so mad as to dance to their pipe to surrender him up into their hands.

Bacon having sent Bland and the rest to do this service, once more re-enters upon his Indian march ; after that he had taken order for the convening an assembly, to sit down on the fourth of September, the summons being authenticated, as they would have it, under the hands of four of the council of state ; and the reason of the convention to manage the affairs of the country in his absence, lest, as he said, while he went abroad to destroy the wolves, the foxes in the meantime should come and devour the sheep. He had not marched many miles from his headquarters but that news came post haste that Bland and the rest with him were snapped at Accomack, betrayed, as some of their own party related, by Captain Carver ; but those who are best able to render an account of this affair do aver, that there was no other treason made use of but their want of discretion, assisted by the juice of the grape. Had it been otherwise the governor would never have rewarded the service with the gift of a halter, which he honored Carver with suddenly after his surprisal. Bland was put in irons and ill-intreated, as it was said ; most of the soldiers owned the governor's cause by entering themselves into his service ; those that refused were made prisoners and promised a releasement at the price of Carver's fate.

Bacon advances against the Indians.

Carver taken and hanged.

The governor being blessed with this good service, and the better service, in that it was effected without bloodshed, and being informed that Bacon was entered upon his Indian march, ships himself for the western shore, being assisted with five ships and ten sloops, in which, as it is said, were about a thousand soldiers. The news whereof outstripping his canvas wings, soon reached the ears of those left by Bacon to see the king's peace kept by resisting the king's vicegerent. For before that the governor could get over the water, two fugitives were got to land, sent, as may be supposed, from some in Accomack, spirited for the general's quarrel, to inform those here, of the

Sir W. ships himself for the western shore.

same principles, of the governor's strength, and upon what terms his soldiers were to fight. And first, they were to be rewarded with those men's estates who had taken Bacon's oath, catch that catch could. Upon what terms the Acomackians were to fight. Secondly, that they and their heirs for twenty-one years should be discharged from all imposition, excepting church dues, and lastly, twelve pence per day during the whole time of service. And that it was further decreed that all servants whose masters were under the general's colors, or that had subscribed the engagement, should be set free and enjoy the forementioned benefits, if that they would, in arms, own the governor's cause. And that this was the whole truth and nothing but the truth, the two men before mentioned deposed before Capt. Thorp, one of the justices of the peace for York county, after that one Colonel Searsbrooke had more prudently declined the admitting these two scoundrels to the test. Whether these fellows were in the right or in the wrong, as to what they had narrated, I know not, but this is certain : whether the same was true or false, it produced the effects of truth in people's minds ; who hereby became so much distracted in their resolutions, that they could not tell at present which way to turn them- The people's perplexed condition. selves ; while their tongues expressed no other language but what sounded forth fears, wishes, and execrations, as their apprehensions or affections dictated ; all looking upon themselves as a people utterly undone, being equally exposed to the governor's displeasure, and the Indians' bloody cruelties ; some cursing the cause of their approaching destruc- tion, looking upon the oath to be no small ingredient helping to fill up the measure of their miseries ; others wishing the general's presence as the only rock of safety, while others looked upon him as only the quicksands ordained to swallow up and sink the ship that should set them on shore, or keep them from drowning in the whirlpool of confusion.

In the midst of these fears and perturbations, the Governor arrives with his fleet of five ships and ten sloops, all well manned, or appeared to be so, before Sir W. arrives at town, September 7. the town ; into which the governor sends his sum- mons (it being possessed by seven or eight hundred Baconians) for a rendition, with a free and ample pardon to all that would

decline Bacon's interest and own his, excepting one Mr. Drummond, and one Mr. Larance, a colonel, and both active promoters of Bacon's designs. Which is a most apparent argument
that what those two men, before mentioned, had sworn to,
was a mere pack of untruths. This his honor's proclamation
was acceptable to most in town ; while others again would
not trust to it, fearing to meet with some after-claps of revenge.
Which diversity of opinions put them all into a resolution of
deserting the place, as not tenable (but indeed had it been
fortified, yet they had no commission to fight), while they had
the liberty of so doing, before it should be wholly invested ;
which that night, in the dark, they put in execution, every one
shifting for himself with no ordinary fear, in the greatest haste
possible, for fear of being sent after. And that some of them
were possessed with no ordinary fear, may be manifested in
Colonel Larence, whose spirits were so much distracted at his
apprehensions of being one excepted in the governor's act of
grace, that he forsook his own house, with all his wealth and a
fair cupboard of plate entire standing, which fell into the
governor's hands the next morning.

The town being thus forsaken by the Baconians,
**The Bacon-
ians forsake
the town.** his honor enters the same the next day, about noon,
where, after he had rendered thanks unto God for
his safe arrival (which he forgot not to perform
upon his knees at his first footing the shore), he applies himself
not only to secure what he had got possession of, but to
increase and enlarge the same, to his best advantage. And
knowing that the people of old usually painted the god of war
with a belly to be fed, as well as with hands to fight, he
began to cast about for the bringing in of provisions for to feed
his soldiers ; and in the next place for soldiers, as well to reinforce his strength within as to enlarge his quarters abroad.
But, as the saying is, man may propose, but God will dispose ;
when that his honor thought himself so much at liberty, that
he might have the liberty to go when and where he pleased,
his expectations became very speedily and in a moment frustrated.

For Bacon, having done his business against the Indians, or
at least so much as he was able to do, having marched his
men with a great deal of toil and hazard some hundreds of

miles, one way and another, killing some and taking others prisoners, and having spent his provisions, draws in his forces within the verge of the English plantations, from whence he dismisseth the greatest part of his army to gather strength against the next designed march, which was no sooner done but he encounters the news of the governor's being arrived at town. Of which being informed, he with a marvelous celerity (outstripping the swift wing of fame) marcheth those few men now with him, which he had only reserved as a guard to his person, and in a trice blocks up the governor in town, to the general astonishment of the whole country, especially when that Bacon's numbers were known, which at this time did not exceed above a hundred and fifty, and these not above two-thirds at work neither, an action of so strange an aspect, that whoever took notice of it could not choose but think but that the Accomackians either intended to receive their promised pay, without desert, or otherwise to establish such signal testimonies of their cowardice or disaffections, or both, that posterity might stand and gaze at their wretched stupidity. *(Bacon blocks the Governor up In town.)*

Bacon soon perceived what easy work he was likely to have in this service, and so began to set as small an esteem upon these men's courages, as they did upon their own credits. He saw by the prologue what sport might be expected in the play, and so began to dispose of his affairs accordingly. Yet not knowing but that the paucity of his numbers being once known to those in town, it might raise their hearts to a degree of courage having so much the odds, and that many times numbers prevail against resolution, he thought it not amiss, since the lion's strength was too weak, to strengthen the same with the fox's brains; and how this was to be effected you shall hear.

For immediately he dispatcheth two or three parties of horse, and about so many in each party, for more he could not spare, to bring into the camp some of the prime gentlewomen, whose husbands were in town; where, when arrived, he sends one of them to inform her own and the others' husbands for what purposes he had brought them into the camp, namely, to be placed in *(Bacon sends for several gentlewomen into the camp, and for what.)*

the forefront of his men at such time as those in town should sally forth upon him.

The poor gentlewomen were mightily astonished at this project; neither were their husbands void of amazement at this subtile invention. If Mr. Fuller thought it strange that the devil's blackguard should be enrolled God's soldiers, they made it no less wonderful that their innocent and harmless wives should thus be entered a white guard to the devil. This action was a method in war that they were not well acquainted with (no, not those the best informed in military affairs), that before they could come to pierce their enemies' sides, they must be obliged to dart their weapons through their wives' breasts; by which means though they, in their own persons, might escape without wounds, yet it might be the lamentable fate of their better half to drop by gunshot, or otherwise be wounded to death.

Whether it was these considerations or some others, I do not know, that kept their swords in their scabbards; but this is manifest, that Bacon knit more knots by his own head in one day than all the hands in town were able to untie in a whole week, while these ladies' white aprons became of greater force to keep the besieged from falling out than his works, a pitiful trench, had strength to repel the weakest shot that should have been sent into his league, had he not made use of this invention.

For it is to be noted that right in his front, where he was to lodge his men, the governor had planted three great guns for to play point blank upon his men, as they were at work, at about one hundred or one hundred and fifty paces distance; and then again, on his right hand, almost close aboard the shore, lay the ships, with their broadsides, to thunder upon him if he should offer to make an onslaught, this being the only place, by land, for him to make his entry into the town. But for your better satisfaction, or rather those whom you may show this narrative to, who have never been upon the place, take this short description.

The place on which the town is built is a perfect peninsula, or tract of land almost wholly encompassed with water, having on the south side the river (formerly Powheten, now called James

The descrip-
tion of James-
town.

river), three miles broad, encompassed on the north, from the east point, with a deep creek, ranging in a semicircle to the west, within ten paces of the river ; and there, by a small isthmus, tacked to the continent. This island (for so it is denominated) hath for longitude, east and west, near upon two miles, and for latitude about half so much, bearing in the whole compass about five miles, little more or less. It is low ground, full of marshes and swamps, which make the air, especially in the summer, insalubrious and unhealthy. It is not at all replenished with springs of fresh water, and that which they have in their wells is brackish, ill-scented, penurious, and not grateful to the stomach ; which render the place improper to endure the commencement of a siege. The town is built much about the middle of the south line, close upon the river, extending east and west, about three quarters of a mile ; in which is comprehended some sixteen or eighteen houses, most, as is the church, built of brick, fair and large ; and in them about a dozen families, for all the houses are not inhabited, getting their livings by keeping of ordinaries, at extraordinary rates.

The governor, understanding that the gentlewomen at the league were, by order, drawn out of danger, resolved if possible to beat Bacon out of his trench ; which he thought might easily be performed, now that his guardian angels had forsaken his camp. For the effecting of which he sent A sally made upon Bacon. forth seven hundred or, as they say, eight hundred of his Accomackians, who (like scholars going to school) went out with heavy hearts, but returned home with light heels ; thinking it better to turn their backs upon that storm, that their breasts could not endure to struggle against, for fear of being galled in their sides, or other parts of their bodies, through the sharpness of the weather ; which, after a terrible noise of thunder and lightning out of the east, began to blow with a powder and some lead, too, as big as musket bullets, full in their faces, and that with so great a violence that some of them were not able to stand upon their legs, which made the rest betake themselves to their heels, as the only expedient to save their lives ; which some amongst them had rather to have lost, than to have owned their safety at the price of such dishonorable rates.

The governor was extremely disgusted at the ill management of this action, which he expressed in some passionate terms, against those who merited the same. But in earnest, who could expect the event to be otherwise than it was, when at the first notice given for the designed sally to be put in execution, some of the officers made such crabbed faces at the report of the same, that the gunner of York fort did proffer to purchase, for any that would buy, a colonel's or a captain's commisssion for a chunk of a pipe.

The next day Bacon orders three great guns to be brought into the camp, two whereof he plants upon his trench. The one he sets to work (playing, some call it, who take delight to see stately structures beaten down, and men blown up into the air like shuttle-cocks) against the ships, the other against the entrance into the town, for to open a passage to his intended storm, which now was resolved upon, as he said, and which was prevented by the governor's forsaking the place and shipping himself once more to Accomack, taking along with him all the townpeople and their goods, leaving all the great guns nailed up and the houses empty for Bacon to enter at his pleasure, and which he did the next morning before day; where, contrary to his hopes, he met with nothing that might satisfy either himself or soldiers' desires, except a few horses, two or three cellars of wine, and some small quantity of Indian corn, with a great many tanned hides.

The Governor leaves town.

The governor did not presently leave James river, but rested at an anchor some twenty miles below the town, which made Bacon entertain some thoughts that either he might have a desire to reënter his late-left quarters, or return and block him up as he had Sir William. And that there was some probability Sir William might steer such a course was news from Potomack, a province within the north verge of Virginia, that Colonel Brent was marching at the head of one thousand soldiers toward town in vindication of the governor's quarrel. The better to prevent Sir William's designs, if he had a desire to return, and to hinder his conjunction with Brent, after he had consulted with his cabinet council, he, in the most barbarous manner, converts the whole town into flames, cinders, and ashes, not

Bacon sets the town on fire.

so much as sparing the church, the first that ever was in
Virginia.

Having performed this flagitious and sacriligious action
(which put the worst of spirits into a horrid consternation at
so inhuman a fact), he marches his men to the Green Spring
(the governor's house, so named), where having stayed,
feasting his army at the governor's cost, two or three days,
until he was informed of Sir William's motion, he
wafts his soldiers over the river at Tindell's Point Goes over into
Gloster.
into Gloster county, taking up his headquarters
at Colonel Warner's; from whence he sends out his mandates
through the whole county to give him a meeting at the court-
house, there to take the engagement that was first promoted
at the middle plantation; for as yet, in this county, it was not
admitted. While he was sedulously contriving this affair, one
Captain Potter arrived in post haste from Rappahannock with
news that Colonel Brent was advancing fast upon him, with a
resolution to fight him, at the head of one thousand men, what
horse what foot, if he durst stay the commencement. He had
no sooner read the letter, when he commands the
drums to beat for the gathering of his soldiers under Bacon resolves
to fight Brent.
their colors, which being done, he acquaints them
with Brent's numbers and resolutions to fight, and then
demands theirs; which was cheerfully answered in the affirma-
tive with shouts and acclamations, while the drums thundered a
march to meet the promised conflict, the soldiers with abundance
of cheerfulness disburdening themselves of all impediments to
expedition, order, and good disciplining, excepting their oaths
and wenches.

Bacon had not marched above two or three days' journey
(and those but short ones, too, as being loth to tire his laborers
before they came to their work), when he meets
news in post haste that Brent's men, not soldiers, Brent's men
forsake him.
had all run away and left him to shift for himself.
For they, having heard that Bacon had beaten the governor
out of the town, began to be afraid, if they should come
within his reach, that he might beat them out of their lives,
and so resolved not to come near him. Colonel Brent was
mightily astonished at the departure of his followers, saying
that they had forsaken the stoutest man and ruined the fairest

estate in Virginia, which was by their cowardice or disaffections exposed to the mercy of the Baconians. But they being, as they thought, more obliged to look after their own concerns and lives than to take notice either of his valor or estate, or of their own credits, were not to be wrought upon by anything that he could do or say contrary to their own fancies.

This business of Brent's having (like the hogs the devil sheared) produced more noise than wool, Bacon, according to summons, meets the Gloster men at the court house, where appeared some six or seven hundred horse and foot, with their arms. After that Bacon, in a long harangue, had tendered them the engagement (which as yet they had not taken, and now was the only cause of this convention), one Mr. Cole offered the sense of all the Gloster men there present, which was summed up in their desires not to have the oath imposed upon them, but to be indulged the benefit of neutrality. But this he would not grant, telling of them that in this, their request, they appeared like the worst of sinners, who had a desire to be saved with the righteous, and yet would do nothing whereby they might obtain their salvation, and so offered to go away, when one Colonel Gouge, of his party, calls to him and told him that he had only spoken to the horse, meaning the troopers, and not to the foot. Bacon, in some passion, replied, he had spoken to the men and not to the horses, having left that service for him to do, because one beast would best understand the meaning of another. And because a minister, one Mr. Wading, did not only refuse to take the engagement, but encouraged others to make him their example, Bacon committed him to the guard, telling of him that it was his place to preach in the church, not in the camp. In the first he might say what he pleased, but in the last he was to say no more than what should please him, unless he could fight to better purpose than he could preach.

The Gloster men, having taken the engagement (which they did not until another meeting, and in another place), and all the work done on this side the western shore, Bacon thought it not amiss, but worth his labor, to go and see how the Accomackians did. It must be confessed that he was a gentleman of a liberal education, and so, consequently, must

The oath tendered to the Gloster men.

Mr. Wading, a minister, imprisoned.

be replenished with good manners, which enables and obligeth all civil persons both to remember and repay received courtesies, which made him not to forget those kindnesses the Accomackians bestowed, in his absence, on his friends and their neighbors, the Virginians. And so now he resolved, since he had nothing else to do, for to go and repay their kind-hearted visit. But first he *Bacon designs to go to Accomack.* thought good to send them word of his good meaning, that they might not plead want of time, for want of knowledge, to provide a reception answerable to his quality and attendance. This was pretty fair play, but really the Accomackians did not half like it. They would rather his honor would have had the patience to have staid until he had been invited, and then he should have been much more welcome. But this must not hinder his journey; if nothing else intervened they must be troubled with a troublesome guest, as their neighbors had been, for a great while together, to their extraordinary charge and utter undoing.

But their kind and very merciful fate, to whom they and their posterity must ever remain indebted, observing their cares and fears, by an admirable and ever to be celebrated providence, removed the causes. For Bacon, having for some time been besieged by sickness, and now not able to hold out any longer, all his strength and provisions being spent, surrendered up that fort he was no longer *Bacon dies October first.* able to keep, into the hands of that grim and all-conquering captain, Death; after that he had implored the assistance of the above-mentioned minister, for the well-making his articles of rendition. The only religious duty, as they say, he was observed to perform during these intrigues of affairs, in which he was so considerable an actor and so much concerned, that rather than he would decline the cause, he became so deeply engaged in the first rise thereof, though much urged by arguments of dehortations by his nearest relations and best friends, that he subjected himself to all those inconveniences that, singly, might bring a man of a more robust frame to his last home.

After he was dead he was bemoaned in the following lines, drawn by the man who waited upon his person, as it is said, and who attended his corpse to its burial place; but where deposited until the general day, not known, only to those who are resolutely silent in that particular. There were many copies of verses made after his departure, calculated to the latitude of their affections who composed them. As a relish taken from both appetites, I have here sent you a couple.

BACON'S EPITAPH, MADE BY HIS MAN.

Death, why so cruel! what, no other way
To manifest thy spleen, but thus to slay
Our hopes of safety, liberty, our all,
Which, through thy tyranny, with him must fall
To its late chaos? Had thy rigid force
Been dealt by retail, and not thus in gross,
Grief had been silent. Now we must complain,
Since thou, in him, hast more than thousand slain;
Whose lives and safeties did so much depend
On him their life, with him their lives must end.
If it be sin to think Death bribed can be,
We must be guilty; say 't was bribery
Guided the fatal shaft. Virginia's foes,
To whom for secret crimes just vengeance owes
Deserved plagues, dreading their just desert,
Corrupted Death by Parasscellcian art
Him to destroy, whose well-tried courage such,
Their heartless hearts, nor arms nor strength could touch.
Who now must heal those wounds, or stop that blood,
The heathen made, and drew into a flood?
Who is it must plead our cause? nor trump, nor drum,
Nor deputations; these, alas, are dumb,
And cannot speak. Our arms (though ne'er so strong)
Will want the aid of his commanding tongue,
Which conquered more than Cæsar. He o'erthrew
Only the outward frame; this could subdue
The rugged works of nature. Souls replete
With dull chill could he animate with heat
Drawn forth of reason's 'lembic. In a word,
Mars and Minerva both in him concurred,
For arts, for arms, whose pen and sword alike,
As Cato's did, may admiration strike
Into his foes; while they confess withal
It was their guilt styled him a criminal.
Only this difference does from truth proceed,
They in the guilt, he in the name must bleed.
While none shall dare his obsequies to sing
In deserved measures, until time shall bring
Truth crowned with freedom and from danger free

To sound his praises to posterity.
Here let him rest, while we this truth report:
He 's gone from hence unto a higher Court,
To plead his cause where he by this doth know
Whether to Cæsar he was friend or foe.

UPON THE DEATH OF G. B.

Whether to Cæsar he was friend or foe?
Pox take such ignorance, do you not know?
Can he be friend to Cæsar, that shall bring
The arms of hell to fight against the king?
(Treason, Rebellion), then what reason have
We for to wait upon him to his grave,
There to express our passions? Wilt not be
Worse than his crimes, to sing his elegy
In well-tuned numbers, where each Ella bears
(To his flagitious name) a flood of tears?
A name that hath more souls with sorrow fed,
Than wretched Niobe single tears e'er shed;
A name that filled all hearts, all ears, with pain,
Until blest fate proclaimed Death had him slain.
Then how can it be counted for a sin
Though Death (nay though myself) had bribed been,
To guide the fatal shaft? We honor all
Who lend a hand unto a traitor's fall.
What though the well-paid Rochit soundly ply
And box the pulpit into flattery;
Urging his rhetoric and strained eloquence,
To adorn uncoffined filth and excrements;
Though the defunct (like ours) ne'er tried
A well intended deed until he died?
'T will be nor sin nor shame for us to say
A two-fold passion checker-works this day
Of joy and sorrow; yet the last doth move
On feet impotent, wanting strength to prove
(Nor can the art of logic yield relief)
How joy should be surmounted by our grief.
Yet that we grieve it cannot be denied,
But 't is because he was, not 'cause he died.
So wept the poor, distressed Ilium dames
Hearing those named, their city put in flames,
And country ruin'd. If we thus lament,
It is against our present joys' consent.
For if the rule in physics true doth prove,
Remove the cause, the effect will after move,
We have outliv'd our sorrows; since we see
The causes shifting of our misery.

Nor is 't a single cause, that 's slipped away,
That made us warble out, a well-a-day.
The brains to plot, the hands to execute
Projected ills, Death jointly did non-suit
At his black bar. And what no bail could save
He hath committed prisoner to the grave ;
From whence there's no reprieve. Death, keep him close,
We have too many devils still go loose.

INGRAM'S PROCEEDINGS.

THE lion had no sooner made his exit, but the ape (by indubitable right) steps upon the stage. Bacon was no sooner
removed by the hand of good providence, but another steps
in, by the wheel of fickle fortune. The country had, for
some time, been guided by a company of knaves, now it was
to try how it would behave itself under a fool. Bacon had
not long been dead (though it was a long time before some
would believe that he was dead) but one Ingram (or
Isgrum, which you will) takes up Bacon's commission, or else, by the pattern of that, cuts him
out a new one, and, as though he had been his
natural heir, or that Bacon's commission had been granted not
only to himself but to his executors, administrators, and
assigns, he, in the military court, takes out a probate of
Bacon's will and proclaims himself his successor.

Ingram takes up Bacon's Commission.

This Ingram, when he came first into the country, had got
upon his back the title of an esquire, but how he came by it
may puzzle all the heralds in England to find out, until he
informs them of his right name ; however, by the help of this
(and his fine capering, for it is said that he could dance well
upon a rope) he capered himself into a fine, though short-lived,
estate, by marrying here with a rich widow, valued at some
hundreds of pounds.

The first thing that this fine fellow did, after that he was
mounted upon the back of his commission, was to spur or
switch those who were to pay obedience unto his
authority, by getting himself proclaimed general of
all the forces now raised, or hereafter to be raised,
in Virginia. Which, while it was performing at the head of

Proclaimed General.

the army, the milksop stood with his hat in his hand, looking as demurely as the great Turk's muftie at the reading of some holy sentence, extracted forth of the Alkoran. The bell-man having done, he put on his hat, and his janissaries threw up their caps, crying out as loud as they could bellow, "God save our new general," hoping, no doubt, that he, in imitation of the great sultan, at his election, would have enlarged their pay, or else have given them leave to have made Jews of the best Christians in the country ; but he, being more than half a Jew himself, at present forbade all plunderings but such as he himself should be personally at.

It was not long before the governor (still at Accomack) had intimation of Bacon's death. He had a long time been shut up in the ark, as we may say, and now thought good to send out a winged messenger to see if happily the deluge was any whit abated ; and whether any dry ground emerged its head, on which with safety he might set his foot, without danger of being wet-shod in blood ; which accordingly he effected, under the command of one Major Beverly, a person calculated to the latitude of the service, which required discretion, courage, and celerity, as qualities wholly subservient to military affairs. And although he returned not with an olive-branch in his mouth, the hieroglyph of peace, yet he went back with the laurel upon his brows, the emblem of conquest and triumph, having snapped up one Colonel Hansford, Beverly takes Hansford. and his party, who kept guard at the house where Colonel Reade did once live. It is said that Hansford, at or a little before the onslaught, had forsaken the capitol of Mars, to pay his oblations in the temple of Venus, which made him the easier prey to his enemies ; but this I have only on report, and must not aver it upon my historical reputation. But if it was so, it was the last sacrifice he ever after offered at the shrine of that luxurious deity, for presently after that he came to Accomack, he had the ill luck to be the first Virginian born that died upon a pair of gallows. When that he came to the place of execution, which was about a mile removed from his prison, he seemed very well resolved to undergo the utmost malice of his not over-kind destinies, only complaining of the manner of his death. Being observed neither at the time of his trial, which was by a court martial, nor afterwards, to

supplicate any other favor than that he might be shot like a
soldier, and not be hanged like a dog. But it was told him, that
what he so passionately petitioned for could not be granted,
in that he was not condemned as he was merely a soldier, but
as a rebel, taken in arms against the king, whose laws had
ordained him that death. During the short time he had to live
after his sentence he approved to his best advantage
Hanford
Executed.
for the welfare of his soul, by repentance and con-
trition for all his sins, in general, excepting his
rebellion, which he would not acknowledge ; desiring the
people at the place of execution to take notice that he died a
loyal subject and a lover of his country ; and that he had
never taken up arms but for the destruction of the Indians,
who had murdered so many Christians.

The business being so well accomplished by those who had
taken Hansford, did so raise their spirits that they had no
sooner delivered their freight at Accomack, but they
Cheisman and
Wilford taken
by Beverly.
hoist their sails and back again to York river,
where with a marvelous celerity they surprise one
Major Cheisman and some others, amongst whom
one Capt. Wilford, who, it is said, in the bickering lost one of his
eyes, at which he seemed little concerned as knowing that when
he came to Accomack that, though he had been stark blind, yet
the governer would take care for to afford him a guide that
should show him the way to the gallows ; since he had
promised him a hanging, long before, as being one of those
that went out with Bacon in his first expedition against the
Indians, without a commission.

This Capt. Wilford, though he was but a little man, yet
he had a great heart, and was known to be no coward. He
had for some years been an interpreter between the English
and the Indians, in whose affairs he was well acquainted, which
rendered him the more acceptable to Bacon, who made use of
him all along in his Indian war. By birth he was the second
son of a knight, who had lost his life and estate in the late
king's quarrel against the surnamed Long Parliament, which
forced him to Virginia (the only city of refuge left in his majesty's dominions, in those times, for distressed cavaliers) to seek
his fortunes, which through his industry began to be considerable, if the kindness of his fate had been more permanent, and

not destined his life to so wretched a death. Major Cheisman, before he came to his trial, died in prison, of fear or grief, or bad usage, for all these are reported, and so by one death prevented another more dreadful to flesh and blood. Cheisman dies in Prison.

There is one remarkable passage reported of this Major Cheisman's lady, which, because it sounds to the honor of her sex, and consequently of all loving wives, I will not deny it a room in this narrative.

When that the major was brought into the governor's presence, and by him demanded what made him to engage in Bacon's designs, before that the major could frame an answer to the Governor's demand, his wife steps in and told his honor that it was her provocations that made her husband join in the cause that Bacon contended for; adding, that if he had not been influenced by her instigations, he had never done that which he had done. Therefore, upon her bended knees, she desired of his honor, that since what her husband had done was by her means, and so, by consequence, she most guilty, that she might be hanged and he pardoned. Though the governor did know that what she had said was near to the truth, yet he said little to her request, only telling of her that she was a w——. But his honor was angry, and therefore this expression must be interpreted as the effects of his passion, not his meaning; for it is to be understood in reason, that there is not any woman who has so small affection for her husband as to dishonor him by her dishonesty, and yet retain such a degree of love that rather than he should be hanged she will be content to submit her own life to the sentence, to keep her husband from the gallows. Mrs. Cheisman's affections for her husband. A kind wife.

Capt. Carver and Capt. Farlow were now, or about this time, executed, as before hinted. Farlow was related to Cheisman, as he had married Farlow's niece. When that he went first into the service (which was presently after that Bacon had received his commission) he was chosen commander of those recruits sent out of York county, to make up Bacon's numbers, according to the gauge of his commission, limited for the Indian service, and by Sir William or some one of the council recommended to Bacon, Capt. Farlow executed.

as a fit person to be commander of the said party. These terms, by which he became engaged, under Bacon's commands, he urged in his plea at his trial, adding that if he had, in what he had done, denied the general's orders, it was in his power to hang him, by the judgment of a court martial, and that he had acted nothing but in obedience to the general's authority. But it was replied against him that he was put under Bacon's command for the service of the country, against the Indians, which employ he ought to have kept to, and not to have acted beyond his bounds, as he had done ; and since he went into the army under the governor's orders, he was required to search the same and see if he could find one that commissioned him to take up arms in opposition to the governor's authority and person. Neither had Bacon any other power by his commission (had the same been ever so legally obtained) but only to make war upon the Indians. Farlow rejoined that Bacon was, by his commission, to see that the king's peace was kept, and to suppress those that should endeavor to perturb the same. It was replied this might be granted him, and he might make his advantage of it, but he was required to consider whether the king's peace was to be kept in resisting the king's immediate governor, so as to levy a war against him, and so commanded him to be silent while his sentence was pronounced. This man was much pitied by those who were acquainted with him, as one of a peaceable disposition and a good scholar, which one might think should have enabled him to take a better estimate of his employment, as he was acquainted with the mathematics ; but it seems the astrolabe or quadrant are not the fittest instruments to take the altitude of a subject's duty, the same being better demonstrated by practical, not speculative observations.

The nimble and timely service performed by Major Beverly, before mentioned, having opened the way

Sir. W. removes to York river.

in some measure, the governor once more sallieth out for the western shore, there to make trial of his better fortune ; which now began to cast a more favorable aspect upon him and his affairs, by removing the main obstacles out of the way by a death, either natural or violent (the one the ordinary, the other the extraordinary workings of Providence), which had with such pertinances and violent perstringes, opposed his most auspicious proceedings. The last time he came, he made choice of James river ; now he was resolved to set up his rest in York, as having the nearest vicinity to Gloster county (the river only interposing between it and York) in which, though the enemy was the strongest (as desiring to make it the seat of the war in regard of several local conveniences), yet in it he knew that his friends were not the weakest, whether we respect number or furniture. It is true they had taken the engagement, as the rest had, to Bacon ; but he being dead, and the engagement, being only personal, was laid in the grave with him, for it was not made to himself, his heirs, executors, administrators, and assigns ; if otherwise, it might have been indued with a kind of immortality, unless the sword, or juster or greater power might happen to wound it to death. But, however, Bacon being dead, and with him his commission, all those who had taken the engagement were now at liberty to go and choose themselves another master.

But though his honor knew that though they were discharged from the binding power of the oath, yet they were not free from the commanding power of those men that were still in arms, in pursuance of those ends for which the engagement was pretended to be taken ; and that before this could be effected, those men must first be beaten from their arms, before the other could get their heels at liberty, to do him any service. Therefore he began to cast about how he might remove those blocks which stood in the Gloster men's way ; which being once done, it must take away all pretences, and leave them without all excuse, if they should offer to sit still, when he and his good providence together had not only knocked off their shackles, but either imprisoned their jailors or tied them up to the gallows.

He had with him now in York river four ships, besides two or three sloops. Three of the ships he *The strength Sir Will. had,* brought with him from Accomack ; the other (a *at his coming to York.* merchantman, as the rest were) was some time before arrived out of England, and in these about 150 men, at his immediate command ; and no more he had when he came into York river. Where, being settled in consultation with his friends, for the managing of his affairs, to the best advantage, he was informed that there was a party of the Baconians (for so they were still denominated, on that side, for distinction's sake) that had settled themselves in their winter quarters, at the house of one Mr. Howards, in Gloster county.

For to keep these vermin from breeding, in their warm kennel, he thought good, in time, for to get them ferreted out. For the accomplishment of which piece of service, he very secretly despatcheth away a select number under the conduct of Major Beverly, who very nimbly performed the same, having the good fortune, as it is said, to catch them all asleep. And lest the good man of the house should forget this good service, that Beverly had done him, in removing his (to him) chargeable guest, with these sleepers, he conveys a good quantity of their landlord's goods aboard ; the Baconians, whereof one a lieutenant-colonel, to remain prisoners, and the goods to be divided amongst those whose service had made them such, according to the law of arms ; which Howard will have to be the law of *harms*, by placing the first letter of his name before the vowel a.

Beverly sur- priseth Col. Harris, in Gloster.

But in earnest, and to leave jesting, Howard did really think it hard measure, to see that go out of his store, by the sword, which he intended to deliver out by the ell or yard. Neither could his wife half like the market, when she saw the chapmen carry her daughter's husband away prisoner, and her own fine clothes going into captivity, to be sold by match and pin, and after worn by those who, before these times, were not worth a point ; yet it is thought that the old gentlewoman was not so much concerned that her son-in-law was made a prisoner as her daughter was vexed, to see they had not left one man upon the plantation, to comfort neither herself nor mother.

This block (and no less was the commander of the forementioned sleepers) being removed out of the way, the Gloster men began to stir abroad, not provoked thereto out of any hopes of getting, but through a fear of losing. They did plainly perceive that if they themselves did not go to work, somebody else would, while they, for their negligence, might be compelled to pay them their wages ; and what that might come to they could

The Gloster men rise for Sir W.

not tell, since it was probable, in such services, the laborers would be their own carvers; and it is commonly known that soldiers make no conscience to take more than their due.

The work that was now to be done in these parts (and further I cannot go for want of a guide) was cut out into several parcels, according as the Baconians had divided the same. And first at West Point, an isthmus which gives the denomination to the two rivers, Pomankey and Mattapony (Indian names), that branch forth of What soldiers at West Point. York river, some thirty miles above Tindell's point, there was planted a guard of about two hundred soldiers. This place Bacon had designed to make his prime rendezvous, or place of retreat, in respect of several local conveniences this place admitted of, and which he found fit for his purpose for sundry reasons. Here it was, I think, that Ingram did chiefly reside, and from whence he drew his recruits of men and munition. The next parcel, considerable, was at Green Spring, the governor's house, into which was put about one At Green Spring. hundred men and boys, under the command of one Capt. Drew, who was resolutely bent, as he said, to keep the place in spite of all opposition; and that he might the better keep his promise he caused all the avenues and approaches to the same to be barricaded up, and three great guns planted to beat off the assailants. A third parcel of about thirty or forty was put into the house of Colonel At Colonel Bacon's. Nath. Bacon, a gentleman related to him, deceased, but not of his principles, under the command of one Major Whaley, a stout, ignorant fellow, as most of the rest, as may be seen hereafter; these were the most considerable parties that the Gloster men were to deal with, and which they had promised to reduce to obedience, or otherwise to beat them out ot their lives, as some of them (perhaps not well acquainted with military affairs, or too well conceited of their own valor) boasted to do.

The person that by commission was to perform this work was one Major Lawrence Smith (and for this service so entitled, as it is said), a gentleman that in his time had hewed out many a knotted piece of work, and so the better knew how to handle such rugged fellows as the Baconians were famed to be.

The place for him to congregate his men at (I say congregate as a word not improper, since his second in dignity was a minister, who had laid down the miter and taken up the helmet) was at one Major Pate's (in whose house Bacon had surrendered up both life and commission ; the one to him that gave it, the other to him that took it), where there appeared men enough to have beaten all the rebels in the country, only with their axes and hoes, had they been led on by a good overseer.

I have either heard, or have read, that a complete general ought to be owner of these three induements : *The properties of a good general.* wisdom to foresee, experience to choose, and courage to execute. He that wants the two last can never have the first, since a wise man will never undertake more than he is able to perform ; he that hath the two first, wanting the last, makes but a lame commander, since courage is an inseparable adjunct to the bare name of a soldier, much more to a general ; he that wants the second, having the first and the last, is no less imperfect than the other, since without experience, wisdom and courage, like young doctors, do but grope in the dark or strike by guess.

Much about the time that the Gloster men mustered at M. Pate's, there was a rising in Middlesex *A rising in Middlesex.* upon the same account ; who were no sooner got upon their feet, but the Baconians resolved to bring them on their knees. For the effecting of which Ingram *Walklett sent to suppress it.* speeds away one Walklett, his lieutenant-general, a man much like the master, with a party of horse, to do the work. M. L. Smith was quickly informed upon what errand Walklett was sent, and so, with a generous *Smith marches after Walklett.* resolution, resolves to be at his heels, if not beforehand with him, to help his friends in their distress.

And because he would not altogether trust to others in affairs of this nature, he advanceth at the head of his own troops (what horse, what foot for number, is not in my intelligence), leaving the rest for to fortify Major Pate's house, and so speeds after Walklett, who, before Smith could reach the required distance, had performed his work, with little labor, and hearing of Smith's advance, was preparing to give him a reception answerable to his designments ; swearing to fight him though Smith should outnumber him cent per cent ; and was not this a daring resolution of a boy that hardly ever saw a sword, but in a scabbard?

In the meantime that this business was a doing, Ingram, understanding upon what design M. L. Smith was gone about, by the advice of his officers strikes in between him and his new-made and new-manned garrison at M. Pate's. **Ingram takes the Gloster men at M. Pate's.** He very nimbly invests the house, and then summons the soldiers, then under the command of the aforesaid minister, to a speedy rendition, or otherwise to stand out to mercy, at their utmost peril. After some tos and fros about the business, quite beyond his text, the minister accepts of such articles, for a surrender, as pleased Ingram and his mermidons to grant.

Ingram had no sooner done this job of journey work, of which he was not a little proud, but M. L. Smith, having retracted his march out of Middlesex, as thinking it little less than a disparagement to have anything to do with Walklett, was upon the back **M. L. Smith retracts his march from Walklett.** of Ingram before he was aware, and at which he was not a little daunted, fearing that he had beat Walklett to pieces in Middlesex. But he, perceiving that the Gloster men did not wear in their faces the countenances of conquerors, nor their clothes the marks of any late engagement, being free from the honorable stains of wounds and gun-shot, he began to hope the best, and the Gloster men to fear the worst; and what the property of fear is, let Felthan tell you, who saith, that if courage be a good orator, fear is a bad counselor and a worse engineer. For instead of erecting, it beats and batters down all bulwarks of defense, persuading the feeble heart that there is no safety in armed troops, iron gates, nor stone walls. In opposition of which passion I will oppose the properties of its antithesis, and say, that as some men are never valiant but in the midst of discourse, so others never manifest their courage but in the midst of danger; never more alive than when in the jaws of death, crowded up in the midst of fire, smoke, swords, and guns; and then not so much laying about them through desperation, or to save their lives, as through a generosity of spirit, to trample upon the lives of their enemies.

For the saving of powder and shot, or rather through the before-mentioned generosity of courage, one Major Bristow, on

Smith's side, made a motion to try the equity and
justness of the quarrel by single combat; Bristow
proffering himself against anyone, being a gen-

Maj. Bristow's challenge to Ingram.

tleman on the other side. This was noble, and
like a soldier. This motion, or rather challenge, was as
readily accepted by Ingram, as proffered by Bristow; Ingram
swearing the newest oath in fashion that he would be the
man, and so advanceth on foot, with sword and pistol, against
Bristow, but was fetched back by his own men, as doubting
the justness of their cause, or in consideration of the disparity
that was between the two antagonists. For though it might
be granted that in a private condition Bristow was the better
man, yet now it was not to be allowed, as Ingram was entitled.

This business not fadging, between the two champions, the
Gloster men began to entertain strange and new resolutions,
quite retrograde to their pretentions, and what was by all good
men expected from the promising aspects of this their league-
ing against a usurping power. It is said that a good cause and
a good deputation is a lawful authority for any man to fight
by; yet neither of these, jointly nor severally, hath a coercive
power to make a man a good soldier. If he wants courage,
though he is enlisted under both, yet is he not sterling coin;
he is at best but copper, stamped with the king's impress, and
will pass for no more than his just value. As to a good cause,
doubtless they had satisfied themselves as to that, else what
were they at this time a contending for, and for

The Gloster men submit to Ingram.

whom? And as for a good deputation, if they
wanted that, wherefore did they so miserably befool
themselves, as to run into the mouths of their enemies, and there to stand still like a company of sheep, with
the knife at their throats, and never so much as offer to bleat
for the saving of their lives, liberties, estates, and what to
truly valiant men is of greater value than these, their credits?
all which now lay at the mercy of their enemies, by a tame
surrender of their arms and persons into the hands of Ingram,
without striking one stroke, who having made all the chief
men prisoners, excepting those who first run away, he dis-
missed the rest to their own abodes, there to sum up the
number of those that were either slain or wounded in this
service.

Much about this time, of the Gloster business, his honor sends abroad a party of men, from off aboard, under the command of one Hubert Farrill, to ferret out a company of the rebels who kept guard at Colonel Bacon's, under the power of Major Whaley, before mentioned. Colonel Bacon himself and one Colonel Ludwell came along with Farrill, to see to the management of the enterprise, about which they took all possible care, that it might prove fortunate. For they had no sooner resolved upon the onset, but they consult on the manner, which was to be effected by a generosity parallel with the design, which required courage and expedition; and so concludes not to answer the sentries by firing, but to take, kill, or drive them up to their avenues, and then to enter pell-mell with them into the house. This method was good, had it been as well executed as contrived. But the sentry had no sooner made the challenge with his mouth, demanding who comes there, but the other answer with their muskets, which seldom speak the language of friends, and that in so loud a manner that it alarmed those in the house to a defense, and then into a posture to sally out. Which the others perceiving, contrary to their first orders, wheel off from the danger, to find a place for their security, which they in part found behind some out-buildings, and from whence they fired one upon the other, giving the bullets leave to grope their own way in the dark (for as yet it was not day), till the general was shot through his loins; and in his fate all the soldiers, or the greater part, through their hearts now sunk into their heels, which they were now making use of instead of their hands, the better to save their jackets, of which they had been certainly stript had they come under their enemies' fingers, who knows better how to steal than fight, notwithstanding this uneven cast of fortune's malice; being a conflict in which the losers have cause to repent and the winners faith to give God thanks, unless with the same devotion thieves do when that they have stripped honest men out of their money. Here was none but their general killed, whose commission was found dripping wet with his own blood, in his pocket; and three or four taken prisoners; what wounded not known, if any, in their backs, as their enemies say, who gloried more in their conquest than ever Scan-

Farrill attempts the Baconians under Whaley's command.

Farrill killed.

derbeg did for the greatest victory he ever obtained against the Turks. If Sir William's cause was no better than his fortunes hitherto, how many proselytes might his disasters bring over to the other side ? But God forbid that the justice of all quarrels should be estimated by their events.

Yet here in this action, as well as some others before, who can choose but deplore the strange fate that the governor was subjected to, in the evil choice of his chief commanders, for the leading on his military transactions ; that when his cause should come to a day of hearing, they should want courage to put in their plea of defense against their adversary's arguments, and pitifully to stand still and see themselves non-suited in every sneaking adventure or action that called upon their generosity, if they had had any, to vindicate their indubitable pretences against an usurped power.

It is true Whaley's condition was desperate, and he was resolved that his courage should be conformable and as desperate as his condition. He did not want intelligence how Hansford and some others were served at Accomack, which made him think it a great deal better to die like a man than be hanged like a dog, if that his fate would but give him the liberty of picking as well as he had taken the liberty of stealing, of which unsoldierlike quality he was foully guilty. But let Whaley's condition be never so desperate, and that he was resolved to manage an opposition against his assailant according to his condition, yet those in the house with him stood upon other terms, being two-thirds (and the whole exceeded not forty) pressed into the service, much against their will ; and had a greater antipathy against Whaley than they had any cause for to fear his fate if he, and they too, had been taken. As for that objection, that Farrill was not, at this time, fully cured of those wounds he received in the sally at town, which in this action proved detrimental both to his strength and courage, why then, if it was so, did he accept of this employ, he having the liberty of refusing, since none could be better acquainted with his own condition, either for strength or courage, than himself. Certainly, in this particular Farrill's foolish ostentation was not excusable, nor Sir William without blame to comply with his ambition, as he had no other parts to prove himself a soldier than a harebrained

resolution to put himself forward in those affairs he had no
more acquaintance with than what he had heard people talk
of. For the failure of this enterprise, which must wholly be
referred to the breach he made upon their sedulous determina-
tions, which was, as is intimated before, to crowd into the
house with the sentry, not only injurious to their own party,
by letting slip so fair an occasion to weaken the power of the
enemy by removing Whaley out of the way, who was esteemed
the most considerable person on that side, but it was and did
prove of bad consequence to the adjacent parts, where he kept
guard. For, whereas before he did only take aim where he
might do mischief, he now did mischief without taking aim ;
before this unhappy conflict he did level at this or that particular only, but now he shot at rovers, let the same light where
it would, he mattered not.

Captain Grantham had now been some time in
Yorke river. A man unto whom Virginia is very Ingram
much beholden for his neat contrivance, in bringing reduced by
Ingram and some others over to harken to reason. Grantham.
With Ingram he had some small acquaintance, for it was in his
ship that he came to Virginia ; and so resolved to try if he might
not do that by words which others could not accomplish with
swords. Now, although he knew that Ingram was the point
where all the lines of his contrivance were for to center, yet he
could not tell, very well, how to obtain this point. For although
he did know that Ingram, in his private condition, was accos-
table enough ; yet since the titmouse (by one of fortune's
figures) was become an elephant, he did not know but that his
pride might be as immense as his power ; since the peacock,
though bred upon a dunghill, is no less proud of his fine
feathers than the princely eagle is of his noble courage. What
arguments Grantham made use of, to wring the sword out of
Ingram's hand, to me is not visible, more than what he told me
of ; which I think was not mercurial enough, against an ordinary
Sophister. But to speak the truth, it may be imagined that
Grantham, at this time, could not bring more reasons to convince Ingram, than Ingram had in his own head to convince
himself ; and so did only await some favorable overtures (and
such as Grantham might, it is possible, now make) to bring
him over to the other side. Neither could he apprehend more

reason in Grantham's arguments than in his own affairs, which
now provoked him to dismount from the back of that horse
which he wanted skill and strength to manage, especially there
being some of his own party waiting an opportunity to toss
him out of the saddle of his new mounted honors, and of
whose designs he wanted not some intelligence, in the countenances of his mermidons, who began for to look askew upon
this, their milksop general, who they judged fitter to dance
upon a rope, or in some of his wenches' laps, than to caper
either to Bellonie's bagpipe or Mars' whistle.

But though Ingram was won upon to turn honest in this
thing (thanks to the necessity, which made it an act of com-
pulsion, not a free-will offering), yet was the work but half done
until the soldiers were wrought upon to follow his example.
And though he himself, or anybody else, might command them
to take up their arms when any mischief was to be done, yet
it was a question whether he, or any in the country, could
command them to lay down their arms for to effect or do any
good. In such a case as this, where authority wants power,
discretion must be made use of, as a virtue surmounting a
brutish force. Grantham, though he had been but a while in
the country, and had seen but little as to matter of action, yet
he had heard a great deal; and so much that the name of
authority had but little power to wring the sword out of these
mad fellows' hands, as he did perceive. And that there was
more hopes to effect that by smooth words which was never
likely to be accomplished by rough deeds, therefore he resolved
to accost them, as the devil courted Eve, though to a better
purpose, with never-to-be-performed promises; counting it no
sin to ludificate those for their good that had been deceived by
others to their hurt. He knew that men were to be treated as
such, and children according to their childish dispositions. And
although it was not with both these he was now to deal, yet
he was to observe the several tempers of those he was to
work upon.

What number of soldiers was at this time in
Grantham at West Point I am not certain. It is said
about 250, summed up in freemen, servants, and
slaves; these three ingredients being the composition of
Bacon's army ever since that the governor left town. These

were informed, to prepare the way, two or three days before
that Grantham came to them, that there was a treaty on foot
between their general and the governor, and that Grantham
did mainly promote the same, as he was a person that favored
the cause that they were contending for.

When that Grantham arrived among these fine fellows, he
was received with more than an ordinary respect, which he
having repaid, with a suitable deportment, he acquaints them
with his commission, which was to tell them that
there was a peace concluded between the governor ^{Upon what terms West}
and their general; and since himself had, in some ^{Point was surrendered.}
measure, used his endeavors to bring the same to
pass, he begged of the governor that he might have the honor to
come and acquaint them with the terms, which he said were
such that they had all cause to rejoice at, than anywise to
think hardly of the same, there being a complete satisfaction
to be given by the articles of agreement, according to every-
one's particular interest, which he summed up under these
heads: And first, those that were now in arms and free men,
under the general, were still to be retained in arms, if they so
pleased, against the Indians. Secondly, and for those who had
a desire for to return home to their own abodes, care was taken
to have them satisfied for the time they had been out, according to the allowance made at the last Assembly. And lastly,
those that were servants in arms, and behaved themselves
well in their employment, should immediately receive discharges from their indentures, signed by the governor or
secretary of state, and their masters to receive, from the public,
a valuable satisfaction for every servant so set free (mark the
words), proportionally to the time that they have to serve.

Upon these terms, the soldiers forsake West Point, and go
with Grantham to kiss the governor's hands (still at Tindell's
Point), and to receive the benefit of the articles mentioned by
Grantham; where when they came (which was by water,
themselves in one vessel, and their arms in another; and so
contrived by Grantham, as he told me himself, upon good
reason), the servants and slaves were sent home to their
masters, there to stay till the governor had leisure to sign their
discharges, or, to say better, till they were free according to

the custom of the country; the rest was made prisoners, or entertained by the governor, as he found them inclined.

Of all the obstacles that had hitherto lain in the governor's way, there is not one, which hath fallen within the verge of my intelligence, that hath been removed by the sword, excepting what was performed under the conduct of Beverly. How this undertaking by Grantham was effected, you have heard, though badly (as the rest) by me summed up. The next that is taken notice of is that at Greene Spring, before hinted, under the command of one Captain Drew, formerly a miller by profession, though now dignified with the title of a captain, and made governor of this place by Bacon, as he was a person formerly beholden under Sir William, and so, by way of requital, most likely to keep him out of his own house. This Whisker of Whorly-Giggs, perceiving now that there was more water coming down upon his mill than the dam would hold, thought best in time to fortify the same, lest all should be borne down before he had taken his toll. Which having effected, making it the strongest place in the country, what with great and small guns, he stands upon his guard and refuseth to surrender but upon his own terms; which being granted, he secures the place till such time as Sir William should, in person, come and take possession of the same. And was not this prettily, honestly done, of a miller?

The greatest difficulty now to be performed was to remove Drummond and Larance out of the way. These two men were excepted out of the governor's pardon, by his proclamation of June last, and several papers since, and for to die without mercy whenever taken; as they were the chief incendiaries and promoters to and for Bacon's designs, and by whose councils all transactions were, for the greater part, managed all along on that side. Drummond was formerly governor of Carolina, and always esteemed a person of such induements, where wisdom and honesty are contending for superiority, which rendered him to be one of that sort of people whose dimensions are not to be taken by the line of an ordinary capacity. Larance was late one of the assembly, and burgess for the town in which he was a liver. He was a person not meanly acquainted with such

Greene Spring secured for William.

Short career of Drummond and Larance.

learning, besides his natural parts, that enables a man for the management of more than ordinary employments, which he subjected to an eclipse, as well in the transactions of the present affairs as in the dark embraces of a blackamoor, his slave ; and that in so fond a manner, as though Venus was chiefly to be worshiped in the image of a negro, or that beauty consisted altogether in the antipathy of complexions, to the no mean scandal and affront of all the votaresses in or about town.

When that West Point was surrendered and Greene Spring secured for the governor, these two generals were at the brick house in New Kent, a place situate almost opposite to West Point, on the south side of Yorke river, and not two miles removed from the said point, with some soldiers under their command for to keep the governor's men from landing on that side, he having a ship at that time at anchor near the place. They had made some attempts to have hindered Grantham's designs, of which they had gained some intelligence, but their endeavors not fadging, they sent down to Colonel Bacon's to fetch of the guard there, under the command of Whaley, to reinforce their own strength.

Drummond and Colonel Larance at the brick house at New Kent.

CÆTERA DESUNT.